James Hudson Taylor

The following books published by Hodder & Stoughton and the overseas Missionary Fellowship are acknowledged as primary reference sources

by Dr and Mrs Howard Taylor
Biography of James Hudson Taylor

by A J Broomhall
Barbarians at the Gates
Over the Treaty Wall
If I had a thousand lives
Survivors' Pact
Refiner's Fire

James Hudson Taylor

Pioneer to Inland China

Joan Clifford

Marshall Pickering

Marshall Morgan and Scott
Marshall Pickering
3 Beggarwood Lane, Basingstoke, Hants RG23 7LP, UK

First published in 1988 by Marshall Morgan and Scott
Publications Ltd
Part of the Marshall Pickering Holdings Group
A subsidiary of the Zondervan Corporation

ISBN 0 551 01465 0

Text set in Baskerville by Brian Robinson, Buckingham
Printed in Great Britain by Cox and Wyman, Reading

Contents

For Dr Lili Pang

1

'Going Chinese'

Here goes! James Hudson Taylor looked thoughtfully at the heavy pile of strange clothes before him, then down at his feet. He wiggled his toes. The young Englishman was wearing tough, cloth Chinese shoes, which he had been trying out for a month. They were still not very comfortable. He looked at himself in the looking glass and grinned. What if his mother and sister could see him now!

His head had been shaved, except for one small tuft and this had been dyed a gleaming black; gone were his blond locks. And that very day the barber had plaited James' remaining piece of hair into a long pigtail, known to the Chinese as a queue or bianzi. This, with an extension of black silk cord now hung right down his back.

James shuddered as he thought of his first attempt to dye his hair. He had been making up the thick black colouring and taken down from the shelf a heavy bottle of ammonia. He had thought he had loosened the big cork with care but in the intense heat of that Chinese summer of 1855, a great pressure had built up inside the bottle. The cork was blown from his hand and gas and liquid ammonia spurted over him – face, hands, clothing. The fumes were awful, he could scarcely breathe. Blindly, he had stumbled his way to a water-butt and plunged in. At once, hearing the commotion, his colleague Dr Parker had rushed in and applied treatment. It was not nice to think about. He had been in great pain for a week and even now, several weeks later, when he had applied the dye to his scalp, which was already uncomfortable with prickly heat, his head had felt to be on fire. The problems of 'going Chinese'. But, as he muttered to himself, 'No gains without pains'.

He undressed and laid aside his western clothes; he did not think he would want them any more. He then began to dress carefully, taking up one after another of the strange garments and putting them on, careful to get them in the right order.

Firstly there was a cool cotton shirt, called a han san, which fastened under the right arm and down the right side. Then the han ku, enormous baggy cotton trousers which fastened with a girdle followed by an ankle-length robe of coarse blue silk with full, wide sleeves that seemed to flap about and get in the way. In the winter, he knew, the robe would be exchanged for one warmly padded against the cold. Now came something to protect neck and shoulders, a kind of tippet, with strings tied under the armpits. Over all this went a waist-length outer jacket, called a ma gua, which buttoned right down the front. In wintertime, the jacket would be lined with fur or wadding. Curious, rather shapeless stockings made of calico were next pulled on, up over the trousers and fastened below the knee with garters of blue. He felt terribly hot but supposed he would get used to it. Lastly, the headgear – for indoors, a skullcap with a button of twisted silk and, for outdoors, a crown-shaped hat with an upturned brim.

'And for days like today', he thought, 'I shall choose this' – picking up a cool conical hat of straw. And since James was determined to look as Chinese as possible and knew that westerners' eyes usually gave them away, he put on, rather self consciously, a pair of tinted spectacles with black Chinese frames.

'That's the lot', he thought with relief. 'I'm the complete Chinese man.'

He shuffled round the room in his new clothes, turning and twisting and trying to feel natural. Soon he would think no more of dressing in this way than he had once done in putting on an ordinary western suit.

Why was James Hudson Taylor turning to Chinese dress? Why was he 'going Chinese'? Some-times missionaries and explorer-botanists had done so as a form of disguise, when trying to pass through parts of the Chinese interior where they might frighten people if they wore western clothes, or risk rough handling for themselves.

This was not the reason for the young missionary James on that hot day in Shanghai over a hundred years ago. It was his intention to honour the Chinese people by openly adopting their life-style; he would dress like them, eat like them, use their courtesies and manners, speak like them, and, in time, he believed, think like them and become one of them.

For they feared and ridiculed the westerners – 'barbarians' as they called them, with their 'outlandish clothes' and short hair, and big noses.

James knew he could do nothing about this; he could not change his European nose and blue eyes, but he considered he was going as far as he could. He truly hoped and prayed that the change would be effective.

For a big change it was; not only in his appearance but in the barrier he was now setting up between himself and the merchant quarter of Shanghai and the other ports, and even between himself and the resident missionary community. For at that time, westerners considered themselves to be superior beings and that to 'go native' in any way was to lower oneself. It was a hard thought for James Hudson Taylor that even Christian friends and fellow-workers would look down upon him, but he knew that they would and that he would have to live with this.

In spite of the problems that awaited him, James felt happy and at peace; he had made his decision and taken the first step. Now would come the test. He was to travel part of the way with his colleague, Dr Parker, who was going to live in a new location. James had decided to make the return journey an opportunity to stop and talk to people about Jesus Christ and give out some books. With his new identity, how would he get on?

The pair set out, James feeling rather awkward as he walked along the jetty in his voluminous new outfit. But no-one took the slightest notice of him. It was Dr Parker in his well-fitting European clothes and silk hat that eyes were fastened on.

Dr Parker said goodbye and James was on his own. He decided that it was true that, as a foreigner rather than a Chinese, he would have been accorded more elaborate respect, but at least people were not now afraid of him. He strolled casually through the town; he climbed a pagoda and looked out across Hangzhou Bay. He saw beautiful orchards of mulberry trees in full leaf. He visited two temples and there was no pointing or nudging. He spoke a few sentences to one or two men and they answered him briefly.

James almost danced back to his lodgings in Shanghai; he felt quite optimistic. In a letter to his family in England he wrote that only time would tell if this new change in his life would win men and women and children to Christ. He believed it might.

A few days later, he baptised his first Chinese convert, Kuei-hua.

2

Getting ready

A fascination with the vast land of China had con-
sumed James Hudson Taylor since early boyhood.
He had first heard about this country from his father
and his father's friends, Methodists in the Barnsley
area of Yorkshire. In 1840, when James was eight
years old, even Christian people in England were not
very interested in the idea of taking the good news of
Jesus Christ to such a remote and strange place.
Queen Victoria had reigned for three years, the one-
penny postal service had begun; British merchants
were very enthusiastic about opening up trade with
China, though mainly trading an Indian drug called
opium in exchange for tea and silk. In this year the
first of two wars with China, known as the 'Opium
Wars' took place, bringing no credit upon England.

But an amazing missionary-interpreter called
Charles Gutzlaff had a few years before travelled
boldly up the China coast and had written some
exciting books. These books had been seized on by
James' father and had altered his thinking. He could
not get China out of his mind. He was puzzled that,
on the whole, missionary work had not caught the

imagination of the Protestant churches on any scale. Mr Taylor, a Methodist lay-preacher, was heard to discuss the matter with his friends. He was a keen reader and his young son James shared his passion for these books.

China had many religions, none very active. There was a simple religion, a worship of heaven, with one god. Later Taoism was founded, though it became debased into a system of demons and magic. About five hundred and fifty years before Christ, Buddhism was brought over from India. Muhammad too had followers.

Young James thought China sounded an amazing place, with its ranges of weird-shaped, mist-covered mountains, mighty rivers, exotic pagodas, enormous population and four thousand years of history. As he moved into his teens, he learned more about the country. It got its name from the title of an early Emperor called Ch'in Shih Huang-ti (Ch'in for short). Hence 'Chin-a'.

Some Christians, called Nestorians, had entered China five hundred years after the birth of Christ, but their witness had declined; a huge black marble monument, discovered centuries later, showed however, that they had been quite an influence. Some Roman Catholic missionaries went to China in the thirteenth century and some ventured far inland. They often met with persecution and some were killed.

By the time of the nineteenth century, in which James lived, some Catholic priests were working far inside China, but few Protestants were there at all.

In those days, Catholics and Protestants did not understand one another very well and hardly mixed.

James grew quite dizzy taking in all these facts, but they were to turn out to be very important to him in days to come.

The household at Barnsley was deeply religious and rather strict, but that was the manner of the times and there was a lot of love in the family. Mr Taylor, who was a chemist, might be stern and quick-tempered, but he was also friendly, and they had lots of interesting visitors. Mrs Taylor was a sweet-dispositioned lady who spent much time with her children. She said many prayers for them. From both sides of the family came a love of music and of art.

There were five young Taylors in the family and James' best friend was his sister Amelia, a few years younger than himself. They remained close all their lives.

Boys and girls were not forced by the government to go to school in those days and Mr and Mrs Taylor preferred to have their family educated at home. Mrs Taylor particularly spent hours reading to her children and opening up for them the secrets of knowledge. When James was eleven he did go out to school for two years, but did not much enjoy it. He was not used to the company of so many other boys at one time. Also, he was not very good at sport. He was rather short – in fact he never grew tall – and not particularly muscular and did not enjoy getting into fights. He was considered by his mother not to be very strong but this many not have been absolutely true. In any case, he was not sorry when his parents decided when he was thirteen that he should leave school and continue his education at home for another year or two.

At fifteen he went to work in a bank for a short time. He was feeling rebellious, like many young people in their teens, and perhaps found the atmosphere at home rather too religious and a bit stuffy. He felt constricted. It was great at first to feel grown up and more of a man-about-town. But gradually it dawned on him that he was not much enjoying the company of the other lads at work; he did not like their language and the way they thought and behaved. Perhaps there was more to what Mama and Papa had taught than he had realised. It was all very confusing. He felt moody and restless and rather sorry for himself.

He was perhaps a bit of a loner, though when he made friends he kept them. He liked the company of pretty girls but had little time or money to spend on them.

Like many youngsters, he had come forward when about fourteen and said that he had given his life to Christ, but it was nothing very deep and made little difference to his life. A real decision did not come until James was seventeen. By this time, a slim youth with fair hair and complexion and blue-grey eyes, pleasant but not handsome looking, he had left the bank. He was now learning from his chemist father the principles of pharmacy in the family business.

One day, when work was slack, James was

flipping through his father's books, idly looking for something to read. He did not know what he wanted. Then he found a bundle of religious leaflets which pointed a moral; they usually included, by way of illustration, a sensational story, usually of someone turning from a life of crime, pictured in detail, to one of goodness. James thought he might find such a story and read this and not bother with the moral. He picked one out and took it to his hideout in an old warehouse in the stable yard. Here he settled down and began to read.

The story was over-dramatic. It concerned a poor, sick coalman who was being visited by some church visitors. These Christians were explaining to the coalman all that Jesus had done for him, by the sacrifice on the wooden cross. The sick man in the story had raised himself on his pillow and cried: 'Then it's done!' meaning that God had done all that was necessary to save and help the human race, himself included. 'Yes' agreed the church people. 'It is finished!' They meant that the sick man had only to believe in Jesus, there was no need for him to struggle on alone.

For some reason, this simple story appealed to James and touched his heart.

'Christ has done everything for me', he thought. 'All I have to do is to accept Him into my heart.' There was a minute's silence. Then he thought, 'I will do it.'

This promise that he made to God was really going to stick and it did. He told his mother and sister Amelia straight away what had happened to him. They could see that he meant it. His mother had been praying secretly that something like this would come to him, for she knew that he had been unhappy.

At the same time, James also decided that he would give his life to God especially in service to China. It was as if God had said to him 'Go for me to China.'

A new happiness and a new energy flooded into him. From that time onwards, James never wavered in his determination that one day he would sail from England to tell the Chinese people the Good News. It was to be another four years before this came true.

* * * * * *

James was keen to get started in preparation for the great day. Friends teased him. Said one 'Everything in China is topsy-turvy! A Chinese book begins at the last page and ends on the first; the lines of print run down the page instead of across . . . women often wear trousers and men wear long robes . . . brides wear red, and white is the colour of mourning!'

Many were more helpful. John Whitworth gave James some Chinese versions of the scriptures. James began to make his own version of a Chinese dictionary, too expensive to purchase. This involved a lot of searching out equivalent words and signs in the two languages and entering them into a notebook.

Chinese calligraphy is fascinating. It is very

beautiful to look at when well produced, the elaborate forms are applied with a fine brush and placed on the page with rhythm and balance.

The Chinese do not have an alphabet as we do; the characters, called ideographs, are more like pictures, each picture meaning the same to any Chinese, just as an Englishman and a Frenchman can both understand the picture of a cow. The Chinese have only two written forms and anyone in China can write meaningfully to anyone else. But the spoken forms have many dialects and a man from Canton could probably not understand a man from Peking. About three thousand forms were necessary for reading and conversation, so Hudson had much to do.

John Whitworth also gave him a copy of a magazine published by a group of forward and outward-looking Christians. This was called *The Gleaner in the Field* and its publishers were The Chinese Society. James at once wrote to the Society, informing them that he himself intended to go out to China in due course. In London he met a celebrated German missionary returned from the Far East; he was most discouraging. 'You would never do for China,' he pronounced, 'not with your eyes and nose and fair hair.'

James was not put off. 'God has called me' he said. 'And he knows about my eyes and nose and hair.'

In the meantime, he worked hard in the pharmacy and at his books, acquiring medical knowledge, for he felt sure this would be useful. He also determined to live simply, to save money and also to train his body for a life of hardship. He asked his mother to store his comfortable mattress and he slept hard. He really meant business.

Eventually he felt he had to get away from home, kind and sympathetic though the family was. He must learn to stand on his own feet. He went to work in Hull, in the north east of England, assisting a Dr Hardy in his duties. He lodged in a dingy area called Drainside and fed himself on a deliberately limited diet, mostly brown bread and apples and water. It did not seem to do him harm though naturally he did not put on weight.

James then began a way of life that was to be crucial in later years and was to mark him out from workers in other missionary organisations. He decided that if God had called him and was ordering his life day by day in a certain way, God would look after him with regard to necessities. He would trust God for necessary monies. To test this feeling, he would not remind Dr Hardy when payday was due; surely God would jog the Doctor's memory. But Dr Hardy was very busy and continued to forget and James finally found himself as the days passed with only half-a-crown.

A complication arose. An Irish Catholic, whose wife was sick, asked James to go and pray with the dying woman. Apparently the local priest was asking for a fee of eighteen-pence, which the Irishman could not pay. Reluctantly, James went to the poverty-stricken little home where the family was near to starvation. He wanted to give the man some money, but did not really want to part with the whole half-crown, since it was all he had.

'Why haven't I got some small coins!' he muttered to himself. He struggled with his conscience. Finally, he gave in, and handed the man the half-crown and went away penniless. The man was full of joy and ran for his priest. James heard later that the woman recovered.

When James got home he had empty pockets but a light heart. Before any real emergency arose, Dr Hardy recalled that he had not paid James and handed him an envelope. James considered that God had honoured his decision and from that time onwards, he never worried to excess about money and where it was to come from.

'If you are doing the Lord's work,' he would say, 'the Lord will make it possible.

*   *   *   *   *   *

After a while, James left Hull to live in London with some relatives, that he might continue his medical studies now at the famous London Hospital. It was gruelling work. He often walked to work to save money.

An unnerving thing happened to him, which might have ended all his dreams. As he worked in the dissecting room, among the dead bodies, he got a scratch which turned septic. Hospital and medical care was less advanced then than it is today and such scratches often proved fatal. The surgeon advised him to hurry home and put his affairs in order.

'You are a dead man', he told James bluntly.

James did not think this could be so, since God had

22

called him to go to China. He was determined not to die yet. With prayer and good nursing he survived – to the amazement of the medical staff.

Suddenly he heard from the missionary organisation called The Chinese Evangelization Society which was helping towards his medical fees. They approached him urgently and suggested that he leave the remainder of his training and go out to China at once.

James' links with this Society were always going to be worrying and in time they would come to an end. But they were the means of getting him out to China to do the one thing he had set his heart on. Rapid was the preparation, many the sad partings, especially from his family, but they all knew he had to go. Unknown to him his parents had dedicated him, as a baby, to the work of the Lord. Now was the time. They stifled their pain and tried to put on a cheerful face.

There was one further pang in James' heart. He had gone through an unhappy love affair with a young music teacher, Marianne. She was fond of him but could not see herself suited to the life in China that James had in mind. James was a grown man, a mature young man of strong feelings and affections. He knew he needed a companion for life, a tender young woman to share his future. Evidently Marianne was not the one. On 19th September 1853, James sailed on the *Dumfries* from Liverpool, bound for Shanghai on the Chinese coast. He was twenty-one.

3

In at the Deep End

It was no joke sailing to China nearly one hundred and fifty years ago. The ships were only as good as the master and the crew and the elements would allow. The journey to Shanghai took about half a year – if you arrived safely. The waters were perilous and you were quickly out of touch with other people – no radio links then. The long weeks of confinement without congenial company would be irritating and if you were becalmed, this was tedious.

The crew of the *Dumfries* were a rough, tough lot and James was the only passenger. During the journey he tried both to keep up his own spirits and to witness as a Christian to Captain and crew. Some sailors showed sympathy with his views but none came right out and declared himself for the Lord.

A terrible storm was frightening; the roaring and foaming of the waters, the towering walls of waves, the tossing and turning of the ship, the creaking of the timbers, and the obvious distress of the crew, were almost unbearable. But James found that his faith held and he was even able to offer hope and comfort to the sailors.

Of course there were also normal excitements on the voyage and amazing sights to see. James was fascinated by calm starlit nights on the waters and the glimpses he had of the strange denizens of the deep. But he was relieved when on a foggy Sunday morning at the end of February 1854, they at last began to make way up the yellow muddied waters of the great river that would finally lead them to the port of Shanghai.

James had read widely of China's history and of her people: now he would really see for himself. The Chinese considered themselves to be the very centre of the earth – they called their land 'The Middle Kingdom' – and considered all other living people to be 'barbarians', ignorant and boorish. They had no wish to have anything to do with 'foreigners', whom they designated 'foreign devils'. By the arrangements of a hard-fought political treaty, foreigners were now allowed to live, trade and own property in five ports along the Chinese coast – Canton, Amoy, Fuzhou, Ningbo and Shanghai – but were not allowed to travel further inland. If they did they could be punished by the magistrates, if not attacked by the residents.

People who ignored these regulations were likely to fall foul of the British Consul, the Queen of England's representative in large cities. It would not take Hudson Taylor long to realise that missionaries were often thought by high-ups to be trouble-makers who did not observe the rules and who wanted to alter local ways. Such criticism was harsh and often untrue, but the British government was not primarily interested in the progress of the Christian faith, but in opening up China to trade and maintaining British influence and did not want any aggravation.

James stood excitedly at the rail as the ship made its way up river, with its special English pilot, who had just come aboard, at the helm. The pilot brought dismal news with him.

In the Europe James had left behind, war clouds were looming and soon the Crimean War would break out and cause misery, not least to the many British soldiers who had to go and fight in it. This was the war, though, which produced the nursing reforms of Florence Nightingale and when James eventually returned to England he would find this remarkable woman very famous.

More important to him at the moment was the situation he was entering in Shanghai. China had been ruled from nearly two thousand years before Christ by a series of families called 'Dynasties'. Since the seventeenth-century the Manchus had held power. But to most Han Chinese, they were really a foreign dynasty, from Manchuria.

This was a time of revolution in China. There were many grumblings about the weakness of the Manchu Emperor. Harvests were bad, there was much unrest. Peasants took up arms. A young man called Hong Xiu-Quan became the leader of a new religious movement called the Worshippers of Shangdi. This seemed to be a Christian movement and church people were hopeful about it. But there was much wrong with it and it became infiltrated by members of Chinese secret societies, called Triads, who wanted to use the movement to get rid of the Manchus.

Instead of bringing new peace and joy to the country, a time of bloodshed ensued that was to last for fifteen years. This warlike time was known as the 'Taiping Rebellion'. The followers of Hong were known as 'the rebels' and wore caps tied with a red scarf; the forces of the Government called 'the Imperial Army'. The rebellion was in its fourth year when James arrived in Shanghai. On Wednesday 1st March 1854, he landed.

'At last!' thought James, standing for the first time on Chinese soil. All round him was the hustle and bustle of this busy port, and the voices of the Chinese sounded loud and harsh to him. He quickly noticed that some people were being wheeled around in a sort of wheelbarrow. And, indeed, on the same sort of wheelbarrows, two squealing pigs were tied, upside down, on either side of the central wheel.

Shanghai was an important commercial centre and in the foreign Settlement lived the 'taipans' or 'big bosses' of the merchant companies. The lived in style with many Chinese servants. There were also officials, bankers, members of the armed forces.

The missionaries had no real position, trying to build good relations with both the Europeans and with the Chinese. But they never attempted to conform to Chinese living; there were many problems.

These were now made worse by the Taiping Rebellion, for the rebels had entered Shanghai the year before. There was utter confusion and heavy fighting going on both inside and outside the city. Life was uncertain.

But James had no time for musing; he had to move off and make contact with people whose names he had been given. He felt very much alone. He held three letters of introduction, and these were his only life-line, as he knew no-one personally in the city. By signs and signals he finally managed to get to the British Consulate, where a nasty shock awaited him. One of his contacts had died, a second had left for America. The third, a very slight introduction, took him to the compound of the London Missionary Society, to which he was directed by the Consul. Here he was welcomed by a well-established Society and given temporary refuge. In this Christian setting, he felt reasonably at home. That night, despite the sound of gunfire and feeling very cold, he slept soundly in a real bed and not a rocking, reeling ship's bunk. In the morning, when he awoke, he heard birds singing and he breathed in the fragrance of flowers. He was rested and ready; everything was going to be all right.

*　　*　　*　　*　　*　　*

When James ventured outside the compound the full impact of his new surroundings hit him. Here was the world of Chinese people, with their sallow skins, dark slanted eyes, and high cheek bones and glistening black hair. How they stared at him, this westerner! They stared at his fair hair and skin, at his blue eyes and at his European clothes. And the sound of the strange tongue he had been trying to master for so long struck harshly on his ears; would he ever understand what they were saying? Would he ever be able really to talk to them? Dr Medhurst and Dr Lockhart at the Settlement and other missionary families were friendly and gave him temporary lodging. But he had to find himself a home and this was obviously not going to be easy. He was advised to study Mandarin, the most widely spoken dialect in China and a teacher was found for him. To his distress, no letters from home had reached the Consulate, not any letters of credit from the Chinese Evangelization Society which had sent him and should have been paying him.

It dawned on James that the other missionary societies, so well settled here, thought his whole arrival among them very strange. Here was a very young man (James always looked youthful, with his fair boyish looks); he was from a little-known new missionary agency; he had some medical skill but was not a 'proper doctor'; he was a lay-preacher but not an ordained minister. The Society that had sent him was obviously ignorant and ill-organised, since they had made no proper provision for his needs and seemed to have given him insufficient funds. The other missionaries tended to ridicule the whole affair and were sorry for James and not much impressed by him.

He began to be aware of this. They were very kind to him but he would get off on his own and make his own way. Meanwhile, he pressed on with his studies and spent several hours a day glued to his Mandarin books, till his eyes ached and his head reeled.

He needed some time off. Outside the compound he pursued his interest in botanical specimens. He would order some cabinets to house insects and butterflies. He saw the most beautiful specimens – a black-winged butterfly as big as a small bird; also many attractive wild flowers, some familiar ones like clover, dandelion and buttercup. All these made him feel less homesick.

But all these things were against a violent background, whose impact he had begun to sense. He heard guns firing and saw skirmishes from his window. He saw that the city wall, about half a mile off, was glittering with sentry lights. He walked through a market and later wrote to his sister Amelia of his impressions.

'Such a muddy, dirty place as Shanghai I never did see.' He was still searching desperately for somewhere to live.

Out in the city with one of the Missioners he saw the sad state in which people lived; houses burned, blown up, totally destroyed. As well as preaching, the missionaries gave away rice to the hungry citizens. At the North Gate heavy fighting was going on and the wounded suffering dreadfully. They met some soldiers dragging along some prisoners by their pigtails; they were going to be beheaded and cried out piteously, but James and his friend could do nothing to help. He felt he really was in the thick of things. There was surely work for him to do here.

He must find a proper home. And once again, loneliness struck; he longed for a loving wife.

4

Through Trials to Happiness

After six months at the Settlement, James found a Chinese house to rent near the North Gate. He said grateful thanks to his missionary friends and moved in. It was a rambling place, neglected and draughty, with altogether too many doors and outhouses. It was also rather near to the Imperial camp and its cannons. But now that he was on his own, a strange peace seized James. He could now live in as simple manner as he chose, and work to his own timetable.

With a smattering of the language, he went quietly out and about, distributing Christian leaflets in Chinese and running a little dispensary for sick people. Some were at first hostile to him as a foreigner but gradually his calm friendly manner impressed them and he soon had a queue of patients and visitors.

Another member of his mission, Dr Parker, arrived with his family. Sometimes James went out with the Doctor. The rebellion was moving away from Shanghai but some grim sights remained. Decapitated heads were struck up on the city wall and James shuddered at the cruelty of it. He saw a tiny baby girl floating dead in a pool – she had been cast out because she was not a boy who would grow up to be strong and useful on the land. James felt for the Chinese women. Even the wealthy ones still had their feet bound in the age-old way, to keep them small and attractive, and could only hobble about; the poor ones worked hard and were often to be seen carrying heavy baskets about on yokes over their shoulders.

James enjoyed brief moments of fun, playing his concertina, and feeding two tiny crickets which had been given to him, and which sang curiously; they needed only a grain or two of rice each day.

Keeping roughly within the requirements of the Treaty, James – now known by most Europeans as Hudson – explored towns and villages within a radius of ten or fifteen miles from Shanghai. He went with Joe Edkins, another settlement preacher, on a longer journey to Kashing-fu, an important industrial centre further inland. In December, they set out on what was to be Hudson's first inland evangelistical journey. They were testing the water to see how far they could travel outside the Treaty confines without causing a commotion. They were both excited.

They visited incense-filled temples and climbed towers and looked out over great China. They travelled mostly by waterway and the landscape glided past, with always something new to see. On landing, they were sometimes roughly handled, once grabbed by their hair, but they got away. Always they were stared at, but in tea houses, temples, quiet streets, small shops, they were able to give away booklets and to commend the gospel in a few simple Chinese phrases which seemed to be understood. This was a great thrill for Hudson.

This was the first of eleven long journeys that Hudson made during his first two years in China. He grew increasingly confident; his hard work on the language was yielding fruit. It was marvellous to be able to say something and get a response. His medical skills were appreciated, except in one town where the druggist saw him as a rival and tried to bundle him off.

With another missionary colleague, John Burdon, he went to a large island called Tsungming in the estuary of the Yangtze river. Here they were graciously received by a high official called the Mandarin who gave them help. Very often, in later years, the Mandarin and the scholars, the intellectuals of China – known as 'the literati' – were the most suspicious of them and caused trouble. So far, Hudson had not been bothered by them.

They toiled up a tall pagoda on the island and once more saw the beautiful landscape set out before them. There were the early crops, tended very neatly in the Chinese way like a pretty garden. Here were streams with drooping willow trees. There were villages and hamlets and beyond them the mighty Yangtze, bearing little boats and fine junks with their graceful sails. This was indeed great China, far away from the confines of the treaty ports with their harsh business atmosphere.

This was Hudson's first sight of the unreached

Chinese interior and his determination to explore yet further deepened. Sometimes he went too far, was reported to the Consul and received a telling-off. But he did not let this worry him.

Dr Parker, Joe Burdon and Hudson took a brief holiday in the important city of Ningbo; they were all working at a fierce pace. At Ningbo they met Miss Aldersey, a senior lady who ran a highly-thought of Christian school. She was a character indeed and had on her staff two pretty young sisters for whom she was responsible. They were the orphaned daughters of a former missionary and were called Burella and Maria Dyer. Hudson was naturally delighted to see these young ladies. He was still longing for a young wife and had indeed been in correspondence with Miss Elizabeth Sissons in England, to whom he had been drawn, but alas, her reaction to leaving England for a life in China had been similiar to that of his first sweetheart, Marianne.

Dr Parker was to set up a hospital in Ningbo and remain there. Hudson was sorry to leave him behind and returned rather sadly to Shanghai.

It was at this time that he decided to adopt a Chinese lifestyle and Chinese dress and he never regretted it. He was constantly running out of money and felt that the Society which had sent him did not really understand how expensive things were. They made it difficult for him to draw funds. But he trusted God and stayed calm; sure enough, the essential money came in always just in time. He was firm that he would never get into debt. He began to receive gifts of money from England from a Mr William Berger. Mr Berger was a well-off, successful manufacturer of household starch, who was interested in China missions and was to become a valuable support person back at home and, in time, a personal friend of Hudson's.

Another powerful figure appeared on the missionary scene, called William Burns. He and Hudson soon knew they were on the same wavelength. Burns somehow acquired a permit for extended travels and invited Hudson to go with him on a missionary tour. Burns was experienced as an evangelist and had found an acceptable way of working. When visiting a new area, they began quietly on the outskirts and worked inwards by degrees to the centre of the town, to the more crowded quarters. They preached simply and gave away gospels and booklets. They visited temples, schools, teashops and private houses. In their Chinese clothing, they attracted far less antagonism and Burns noticed that Hudson was very good in a time of crisis and at handling awkward people.

A Christian sea-captain reported the need for some Christian teaching in the notorious city of Swatow. This was a place where foreigners made much money from the sale of the drug opium and also took part in the coolie-slave trade. Not surprisingly, visiting evangelists were under suspicion too and were known as 'foreign dog' or 'foreign pig' and hissed and booed off without ceremony.

Burns and Hudson decided that they must go

there and rented a simple shack in the Chinese quarter. A little Christian seed was planted that in years to come would bear an abundant harvest.

Hudson had to go back to Shanghai for some medical kit. He never saw Burns again but their friendship had been deep. In Shanghai, Hudson found that a fire had destroyed the medical stores and he sought help from Dr Parker in Ningbo. Things were going well there. And of course, the attractive Misses Dyer were still there. Hudson was just about to go back to join Burns in Swatow when he got a mysterious message not to go there on any account. All doors at the moment seemed to be shutting in Swatow. It seemed that Burns had been roughly handled and the Chinese workers put under house-arrest. The British authorities were not keen for Hudson to return. It was not his fault but it seemed as though for the time being he had to stay in Ningbo. Perhaps it was God's will?

Hudson realized he was falling in love with Maria. She had a slight cast in one eye but he found this very attractive. She too was drawn by this quiet yet confident young missionary. But the young lovers had to go through a lot of pain and misunderstanding before they were able to put their lives together. Miss Aldersey, in whose care Maria was, was not at all convinced that Hudson was a suitable match for her charge; she proved very much of a stumbling-block. Maria was of good family, well-connected, with some private means, accustomed to being much sought after. She had several other beaux, some in high positions. Hudson could not be said to have any great future before him, as far as could be seen. He was in no way a catch for Maria. All this Miss Aldersey sharply pointed out to Maria.

Letters to and from relatives and guardians ground slowly back and forth between China and England. Only eventually was permission granted, for Maria was very young. On 20th January 1858, the couple were married in Ningbo, in an old temple above the Consulate. Maria wore a grey silk gown and Hudson his best Chinese suit. Kind friends provided a simple reception and the young married pair went for a brief honeymoon to an old monastery in the western hills.

It was most romantic. They were passionately in love and remained so for the rest of their lives together. At last Hudson had that confidante he had so long wanted, that special person with whom to share everything. His happiness was complete. Maria was one of these fortunate people who had few spiritual problems. Her nature was sweet and calm and to her God always seemed very near.

Having lived in Ningbo since the age of fifteen, she spoke perfect Mandarin, and was the perfect loving support and partner to Hudson. They began their married life in a little room over the chapel in Bridge Street, which seemed to form the cradle of an important missionary organisation as yet unnamed.

In their little sitting room, two beautiful Chinese scrolls now hung, examples of the lovely work of this kind for which the Chinese are famous. The scrolls bore words from the scriptures; in Hebrew they read, *Ebenezer* and *Jehovah Jireh*. Their meanings were: 'Hitherto hath the Lord helped us', and 'The Lord will provide'.

By these scripture words the young couple lived and would continue to do so.

5

The CIM Is Born

Hudson and Maria were blissfully happy in their little home in Bridge Street. Maria taught in the school, making full use of her gifts and training. Hudson preached in the tiny chapel on the ground floor, entertained callers, also gave lessons, and dispensed medicines to sick people. Maria was never in very good health; as she moved into womanhood and later to the birth and care of a large family she, like most European women in China, found the climate and the hardships difficult to endure, but she faced them joyfully.

The young Taylors were overwhelmed with joy when two Chinese workmen accepted Jesus Christ as Lord and turned to the Christian faith. Hudson always believed that the main thrust of the work should be in the hands of the local Chinese people and to bring this about was always his aim. He thought of the Chinese who became Christians as then becoming themselves 'soul-winners' to carry on the good work when the European evangelists had passed on.

Hudson made a series of coloured pictures which

he put up at his Sunday services to help explain the gospel. To these services came Fan Neng-Kuei, a basket-maker who had for a long time been seeking an answer to life's questions and a true faith. He quickly gave over his life to Christ, though it led to some persecution at first in his village. It was costly for him, since he had to give up a working day's pay to attend church on Sunday. But soon, through his witness, another convert was to become a key figure in the Chinese church.

One day a workman called Wang Lee-Djun was decorating a lady's guest-hall when he heard an argument going on around him, between the lady of the house and Fan the basket-maker. Very politely, but firmly, Fan was refusing to make a basket to hold incense for idols.

'I am a Christian, Madam,' said Fan, 'and I cannot have anything to do with idol worship.' He then went on to tell the lady about the life and sacrifice and resurrection of Jesus. The lady shrugged and teetered away on her tiny bound feet, but Wang, up on his ladder was enthralled and climbed down to hear more. Whatever was said to him by Neng-Kuei began something that truly blossomed, for soon Wang became a devoted follower of Jesus and a lifelong friend and servant to the Taylors.

*   *   *   *   *   *

At the hospital in Ningbo, Dr Parker was doing well and had a steady inflow of patients. But, as happened only too often to European women, his wife grew ill and died. Very concerned for his children, the doctor decided to take them back to England. He thought Hudson could manage the dispensary but did not like to ask him to supervise the hospital as well. Hudson believed he could do this and moved in at once. The strain, physical and mental, was too much and Hudson broke down.

Back in England, Mr William Berger had inherited family money and had decided to give more of it to support Hudson. He very much wanted to talk to the young missionary about the future of his work.

Before long his wish was granted. In 1861, Hudson was compelled to leave China for his health's sake and take a break in England. Maria also needed a change of climate. So the money was found for the couple to visit England, with the two children who were now part of the Taylor family and also Wang Lae-Djun, who was their companion and house-keeper.

People in London were surprised to see an English-woman walking down the street in unfashionable Victorian clothes, side by side with two chinamen with long pigtails, each carrying a white baby.

It turned out to be five years before they returned to China. Every minute of their English stay was fully occupied. Hudson decided he ought to complete his medical studies, interrupted all those years ago, and should complete his medical degree. So he enrolled again at the London Hospital and they took a small house nearby in Whitechapel, a fairly poor and deprived area.

Hudson also had another big task to complete, he was going through a translation of the New Testament, turning it into the language of the Ningbo people. He tried to produce simple, everyday words that people would understand and sometimes ran into trouble with learned scholars because of this. He did not want to use long words and literary expressions. This task was rather tedious and not easy for Hudson's eyes, never very strong. Sometimes Maria helped him.

They lived very simply. They received no money from Ningbo and as always had only just enough for everyday necessities. They prayed daily to God to supply their needs and somehow just enough appeared, though never any to spare. A visitor to the Whitechapel house, a young man offering to go to China, was surprised at the bare way in which the Taylors lived.

'The furnishing was very simple,' he told his friends, 'and the table-ware was all mixed up, nothing matched . . .' Such things were of no importance to Hudson and Maria. They showed an utter indifference to physical comfort. They had deeper things on their mind. Also, as their family continued to grow, they had their children's needs to put first.

James Meadows, who had noted the simple furnishings, also spoke of the character of the Taylors.

'There is a gentle, earnest piety about them,' he said.

Hudson was always praying for more European workers to go back to China with him. He himself had no great influence or money to back them. Now that he was a little older and had worked in China, he knew that he was forced to make demands of anyone he took with him. It was always possible that they might even lose their lives! For a while, this worried him, so much so that he could scarcely sleep. He tossed and turned at night, Maria could not seem to help him.

They took a short holiday in the bracing air of Brighton, in June 1865. Hudson went off for a solitary walk by the sea. He was thinking and praying furiously. What if he took young people and they ran into trouble? They could be attacked? What if they ran out of money and grew hungry? Or things could be just too hard for them. He was not sure that he ought to lay such burdens on young people.

Suddenly, a startling thought came to him, 'If we are obeying the Lord, the responsibility rests with Him!' It dawned on Hudson that it was not his job to worry about everyone's future, but to be frank and open with those who volunteered, and to make it clear that they would all depend on God and on God alone.

A weight seemed to fall from his shoulders. He was carrying his bible – he had come from Sunday service – and on the flyleaf he now wrote; 'Prayed for twenty-four willing skilful labourers at Brighton, June 25th 1865.' Then he went back at a smart pace to his lodgings, whistling. He had put all his burdens on the Lord. Maria thought that Brighton had done him a lot of good, and so it had.

The new glow within Hudson had quick and far-reaching results. Two days after his return from Brighton, he went to the bank and opened an account with just ten pounds for, 'The China Inland Mission.'

He had prayed for men and women to go back to China with him; this group should have a name.

The name China Inland Mission was to remind them of their purpose – to take the Gospel of Jesus Christ deep within China, to the millions in this vast land who had never heard of Jesus' name. So the China Inland Mission was born; there was now no going back.

*　　*　　*　　*　　*　　*

Hudson was never a powerful public speaker in the grand manner, shouting and waving his arms about, he spoke clearly and rather quietly and without mannerisms, but there was such conviction and sincerity when he spoke that all coughing and whispering immediately stopped. People focused on the slight, pale figure in the Chinese robes. He was much in demand for speaking and could have gone out doing so every day. He did go to address a huge Christian conference in Scotland, where he was blunt when pleading the cause of the Chinese people.

The congregation had been heartily singing a poetic hymn, 'Waft, waft, ye winds the story', indicating that the wind would blow the Christian gospel to those across the sea. Hudson shook his head. 'No good just singing that', he said firmly, 'the wind will never blow the story, but the winds can blow us . . .' He was thinking of the sailing ship in which he had been going backwards and forwards across the oceans, blown onwards by the wind. He went on to urge people to pray for missionaries who would visit the numbers of Chinese provinces into which no missionary had yet penetrated.

One day, on impulse, he went into a chapel where a group of Christians were praying. He joined in their prayers. His own praying so much impressed one lady that she asked about him and invited him to her house. She was the Dowager Lady Radstock, an influential society lady and she and her family became friends to Hudson; through them help and money came the way of the mission. Hudson could mix with all kinds of people.

Hudson, in his time of prayer, was now boldly asking God to 'thrust forth twenty-four European and twenty-four Chinese evangelists.' A number of young men and women had volunteered to go to China and some had been accepted.

Hudson called them together and made clear the conditions on which they would join him in China. They would 'go out as children of God at God's command, to do God's work, depending on Him for supplies.' They would, 'wear Chinese clothes and go inland.' Hudson made his own position very clear. 'I am to be the leader in China and my direction implicitly followed . . .'

He was no longer the rather reserved, shy young man who had first gone to China thirteen years before; some people thought he was getting a bit high-handed, but he and Maria were the only ones with any experience of the situation that might be met.

'Your only real guarantee' said Hudson, 'is that which you carry between the covers of your Bible . . .'

In spite of their attitude towards gathering money for their funds – praying but not begging – enough money was got together for them to book passage for 1866. Hudson was a lot better but Maria was still frail. They now had four children and knew not what was in store for them. But they believed they were off to do God's will and made their preparations in that spirit. They booked the entire accommodation of the ship *Lammermuir*. They must avoid the expensive overland route via Suez and must travel round the dreaded Cape. They sailed on 26th May 1866. 'Our one desire and aim,' said Hudson, 'is to plant the standard of the Cross in the eleven provinces of China hitherto unoccupied and in Chinese Tartary . . .'

6

The CIM In Action

Steam ships had made their appearance since Hudson had first sailed to China but were still rare. Now was the era of the clipper ships, sailing ships famous for their beauty of outline and increased speed, valuable in rapidly bringing back to England Chinese tea and silk. In 1866 when the party of the newly-formed China Inland Mission set off, a famous and exciting clipper race took place, when the sleek ships ploughed their way through the oceans to gain first arrival.

The *Lammermuir* on which the party sailed was no greyhound like these, but it was a clipper and was expected to made the journey in four months. Voyages of this kind were still dangerous and ships were still wrecked on the treacherous reefs of the East Asian route.

Hudson and Maria banished these thoughts from their minds as they boarded for their historic journey. They had seen all their boxes and trunks and parcels aboard. All the party put on worn-out clothing specially for the voyage, since tar and smuts were expected to affect clothing and make it unfit for further use. The same with bed linen.

After the goodbyes and as the ship left, the whole party burst into a hymn of thankfulness and hope. This fairly startled the crew, a motley crowd of different nationalities with no great opinoin of so-called 'religious people'. The first mate, a bad-tempered, violent chap called Brunton, wrote to his wife, 'We're going to have a whole shipload of missionaries psalm-singing all day long; wish we were out of it!'

However, as the party settled down and found their way round the ship and became accustomed to the drill of ship life, relations with the crew grew friendly. Hudson and Maria had much to do, using the four months of the voyage as a school in which to teach the new young missionaries who were totally inexperienced. Also, Hudson was always ready to give his surgeon's skill when anyone, crew or passengers, fell ill or had an accident, a common occurrence on board.

He was anxious that the party – eighteen adults and four children – should be welded into a harmonious whole. They were all very different; some were scholarly and clever, some were uneducated but devoted. They included a blacksmith, a mechanic, a stone-mason and two carpenters. They were also from different branches of the Christian church, since Hudson did not care about denominations. There were no ordained clergy among them as Hudson did not see the necessity for this. Though they shared a common Lord and a common purpose, getting on together was not going to be easy.

They were cooped up together for four months on the ship. There was some unpleasantness among the party and some difficulties that had to be ironed out. Hudson was amazingly calm and good-tempered, considering his heavy responsibilities.

Everything looked like coming to an end when a fearful typhoon blew up. For fifteen days they were gripped in its terror. So bad were things that the captain bade them all put on their lifebelts – he could see no hope. The crew refused to go on working and taking risks and crowded together in the forecastle. The Captain advanced towards them with his revolver. Hudson hurried over and begged him to put this away. He spoke quietly and calmly to the frightened crew. All the party turned to prayer. Eventually, pretty well everything had gone – sails, masts, everything but their hope in God. They beat up the China Sea all but a wreck, yet they survived. None was missing or seriously injured. It was a miracle.

On arrival in Shanghai, making their way to the foreign settlement, accommodation for this large group must be found. It had not been possible to arrange for anything beforehand. Chinese inns were unsuitable for women and children and hotels far too expensive. Help appeared in the shape of a young American Christian and they were soon all housed temporarily in a lage warehouse, known as a go-down, which while lacking refinements was draught-free and roomy.

A month later they found permanent accommodation in the city of Hangchow. Their new home was a rambling building, formerly a Mandarin's house, in a quiet corner of the city, near the wall. It was a rabbit-warren of a place with plenty of room for living quarters, guest rooms, a dispensary for the medicines, a chapel, a printing press and the necessary servants. They were established: the China Inland Mission was in place.

*　　*　　*　　*　　*　　*

Back in England, thousands of miles away, a supporting base for the Mission was also being established in a new house. This was Saint Hill, the beautiful country mansion of Mr William Berger, the wealthy businessman who was taking such an interest in the CIM. He and his wife, though no longer young, were busy transforming their quiet home into a busy centre for the Mission. They cleared lofty rooms to make offices, store rooms for papers and leaflets and boxes of articles to go out to China. They made rooms available for guests visiting on the Mission's business and to put up young men and women who would be coming to offer themselves as missionaries and who would need to be interviewed and carefully selected. There was as much excitement going on here as out in China.

William Berger was sad to receive a few letters from the Missionary party which were of a critical nature, but he answered them quietly and prayerfully and never doubted that Hudson was right in his leadership. The plain fact was that the young mission workers had taken on a very hard task and some of the facets of this new life were hard for one or two to take.

Adopting Chinese dress and customs, though agreed upon before sailing, was a cause of some argument. Some of the young men did not enjoy this and missed the extreme deference (not always genuine) that European clothes usually afforded their wearers. The young women, when they took Chinese clothing, had also to adopt Chinese ways and these were sometimes felt to be restrictive. Chinese of good standing had stern ideas about how men and women should behave. If a lady went out into the street, she should be accompanied by another woman. Even if she was a married woman, she should not hold her husband's arm in the street. All these customs could be irksome, even to Maria who had never before worn Chinese dress. But Hudson was convinced that this was abolutely vital both in helping them to get alongside the Chinese and also in keeping the workers out of trouble.

Nevertheless, the *Lammermuir* group now living quietly in Hangchow was getting on with language studies and learning Chinese ways. As they lived peaceably together and were heard singing their Christian hymns, gradually the Chinese people wandered into their quarters and gradually lost their fear of the foreigners.

The dispensary was a wonderful tool and Hudson was able to give treatment to many sick people. As the missionaries grew in knowledge and experience, they began to leave Hangchow quietly and go out on journeys to talk about Jesus – this was known as evangelising. The Scotsman, Duncan, went to Huchow; Meadows and Scott went to Taichow and Wenchow. These were important capital cities, known as 'Fu' cities.

One of the young women workers, Jennie Faulding,

quickly took to Chinese dress and managed fairly good Chinese. She was a vivacious, lively girl, full of hope and spirit and ready for any adventures. She began to visit Chinese women in their homes, which male workers could never do. Gradually these women came to the chapel and a small church began to thrive. Jennie was especially good at getting on with the Chinese women and realy loved them.

*   *   *   *   *   *

The summer of 1867 was terribly hot and health weakened and tempers rose. Hudson felt worn out and Maria looked pale and ill. A trip was planned to the cool hills. Here, lodgings were found in the grounds of a ruined temple. It was the most serene area, with pines, oaks and elms giving welcome shade, and mountain streams rippling by.

Hudson and Maria soon felt rested and better but even in this beautiful place illness struck. The Taylor's eldest child, little Gracie, a real little personality, fell ill. She was eight years old, a delightful child very close to both parents. Within a few days, Gracie was dead. This was a heavy blow to Hudson, for Grace had been his constant companion. He wrote to his Mother, 'Our dear little Gracie; how we miss her.' Yet he was convinced that Gracie rested in the loving Heavenly Father's care. He wrote very poignantly to William Berger, reminding him of what Hudson had always known in going to China, 'I laid my wife and children with myself on the altar for His service . . . God has not left us now . . .'

It was a sad return to Hangchow but there was good news of the spread of the gospel. The stone-mason, George Duncan, a strapping great fellow, had made his way to Nanking, a large city which had twice been China's capital city.

He had not been made welcome but had finally found lodgings in the drum tower of a Buddhist temple, among the rubbish and rats. He did not care. He worked at his Chinese by standing beside a man at the wash-tub and repeating usuful phrases. Duncan was no great scholar, but he loved Christ and he loved people. He made his way in Nanking and began a work there that was later to become one of the strongest Christian centres in China.

Hudson was good at finding the right jobs for people. Willie Rudland was another worker who found problems with the language and was getting headaches; studying was not easy for him. Hudson saw his distress. One day he said to Wiliam, 'I'm worried about the printing press, the workmen get through so little work. Do you think you could look after this for me?' Rudland was delighted. The cheerful activity of the printing room was more to his liking and, without realising it, he picked up Chinese phrases more quickly than when sitting listlessly at a table. His headaches soon disappeared and the printing was accomplished more quickly.

Hudson was always a quick thinker. One night, a message from a sick missionary at home brought him hurrying back to Hangchow at a late hour. To his dismay, the gates were barred and closed. As with most large Chinese cities, a strong wall surrounded

Hangchow. Darkness had fallen. How could he get in? Suddenly someone rode past him and shouted and signalled and a large basket was let down over the city wall and the man stepped in. There was not room for two but Hudson's quick eye saw a length of rope hanging from the basket. Without hesitation, he seized it and clung on for dear life.

At the top, some angry guards were not pleased to see him, but he was inside the city.

Later that night, having treated the invalid, he told the story of his arrival.

'What did you say to the guards?' someone asked.

'I gave them two hundred good reasons for letting me in', replied Hudson calmly.

'Two hundred! did you have time for that?'

'Yes', said Hudson smiling. 'The two hundred reasons came out of my purse – and did not take that long.'

In spite of the death of little Gracie, many blessings had crowned the first year of the life of the China Inland Mission. The stations occupied by the Mission had doubled in number and the missionaries were working further and further away from the Treaty ports. With the exception of Hangchow, no Protestant missionaries except those of the CIM were settled anywhere away from the coast and treaty ports.

It was all very exciting.

7

Time of Testing

After a year and a half, Hudson Taylor knew he must leave Hangchow and press on further. The little church there was growing steadily under the pastoral care of Wang Le-Djun and John McCarthy and Jennie Faulding would visit homes and talk to enquirers.

The Taylors, their family, some other European workers and several Chinese, moved to Yangchow. Almost from the first, things were difficult and rather sinister. They had now left the Treaty Ports behind and were attempting to occupy a major city barely touched by missionaries as yet. A lot would depend upon the tolerance of the Governor, Ma Xinya, a Muslim.

Relations with foreigners here were at a low ebb and they received a cool welcome. There was much whispering as they passed and though groups of people came and stared at the house, then melted away, there was a reluctance to come in and visit them. Hudson put all this down to the attitude of the so-called 'thinkers', the literati, Chinese intellectuals of high social class who were afraid of what the foreigners might say or do.

These literati influenced ordinary working Chinese men and women and spread around the most ghastly tales and passed round scurrilous handbills. The most dreadful suggestions were made about these 'foreign devils'; the worst, yet most believed, was that the foreigners kidnapped Chinese babies, killed them, and salted them down to eat in the winter. Also, that they took out their eyes and made medicines from them.

The summer of 1868 was hot and everyone grew fractious. Then one morning Hudson received a note, pushed under the door, and unsigned, warning him that the following day the local people were going to riot at the mission house. 'Be careful,' warned this well-wisher.

There was not a lot Hudson could do, though he called the party together, they said their prayers and decided on the safest rooms for the women and children. They barricaded the doors to their personal quarters and set a guard on each.

Sure enough, the next morning, sounds of people approaching could be heard and on peeping out, a mob of unruly characters was seen coming to the house, armed with knives and staves. Stones began to be thrown. Then it began to rain heavily, something the Chinese disliked, and they went away. Hudson and his party kept quietly to the house, in the hope that the madness would pass. A few days went by.

Then, unfortunately, two white strangers were seen walking openly in the city. They were nothing to do with Hudson's party but that foreigners had appeared was enough. A tale spread like lightning through the city that foreign ships were in the harbour, that twenty-four babies had disappeared, surely abducted by these foreigners, and the ships must all be full of rich treasure, there for the taking.

Inflamed by these rumours, the mob gathered again and this time made a determined attack on the Inland Mission property. They battered at the door, yelling and shouting. They threw things and tried to start fires. The women and children huddled together in an inner room, very frightened, yet composed in their belief that God would protect them.

When darkness fell, Hudson and a friend managed to creep out of the back of the house and make their way rapidly to the dwelling of the Mandarin, the chief citizen. They were chased but ran on and flung themselves into the Judgment Hall, called the 'Yamen', shouting out loudly 'Kiu-ming! Kiu-ming! – 'Save Life! Save Life!' At this cry the Mandarin was bound to attend to them in their trouble.

Gasping, Hudson poured out his story and demanded help. The Mandarin took his time; Hudson was disgusted when the man asked him, 'What did you really do with the babies?' Hudson nearly exploded. 'None of the rioting would be going on now if you had suppressed all these awful lies when they started,' he declared.

The Mandarin nodded. 'Very true, I must first quieten the people and then investigate.'

In about an hour, the Governor, the Captain of the military, a squad of soldiers and two local Mandarins, went to the scene of the disturbance and seized some of the culprits. Looting was going on. At the sight of the property, Hudson was sad. Several attempts had been made to set it on fire, furniture and belongings were smashed and lay about in pathetic broken heaps. The inhabitants had managed to get out. First they had sheltered in a well-house beneath the ground, then they had hurried to a friendly neighbour's house, but not without hurt. The women and children had had to make an unceremonious exit, jumping from a verandah roof. Maria hurt her leg and Emily, another worker, fell flat on her back on the stones and was lucky not to have broken her spine or split her head.

After an exhausting day patching things up, the mob returned. Again Hudson had to get to the yamen and demand help. Again soldiers were sent and some arrests made. The Mandarin, a rather weak man, suggested that the missionary party should leave the area for a time, until the local people had calmed down. Hudson agreed and they crept out quietly and took boats to Chinkiang.

'I cannot attempt to describe to you our feelings,' wrote Maria, 'but God was our stay and He forsook us not.'

At Hudson's suggestion, a large stone tablet was put up outside the Yangchow house, stating that the foreigners inside enjoyed official protection. But when they did return, it was their quiet peaceful attitude, demanding no vengeance, that most impressed the local people. They showed no bitterness and the missionary party simply went on with their loving work. Maria was expecting another baby and chose to have it in the Yangchow house. When local people heard this and peeped in and saw how tenderly and gently Maria and Hudson handled their baby, and how the entire missionary party took turns in tending it, they were most impressed and began to understand that the awful tales they had heard could not possibly be true.

*   *   *   *   *   *

Unfortunately, the episode of the riot was not yet done with. Ripples spread far away and caused trouble. A well-meaning resident in Chinkiang had written to the papers, upset that the missionaries had been so attacked, and this newspaper cutting had been sent to England. Articles soon appeared in the English paper *The Times*, known as 'The Thunderer', and questions were asked and ignorant speeches made in parliament. Once more the missionaries were branded as trouble makers and the Duke of Somerset demanded that all missionaries be made to leave China and return to England – all this commotion, he said, was bad for the British image and bad for trade! There could even be a war! This was very tough on Hudson; he had not asked for gunboats to come up the Yantze to protect him. All he had done was to write a brief pencilled note to the Consul telling him what had happened.

This was an unpleasant time for Hudson and his friends and lasted some while. Mr Berger was struck by Hudson's letter and the 'gentle, humble, tender spirit under trial' that they had shown. Yet Hudson was still asking for more workers to come out – he would not let temporary problems block their progress for long.

* * * * * *

There was a lot of sickness in the Mission, the climate took its toll. It was now agreed that four of the Taylor children should be taken back to England. Emily Blatchley agreed to go with them and to look after them in England. This was painful for Maria and Hudson, but they truly believed that the little ones would be healthier and happier, and perhaps safer, back home. They kissed and hugged their children and then they were gone.

Christians were made, Chinese people baptized and the little church grew. But Maria was seen to be getting thinner and paler and Hudson knew she was a very sick lady. In July 1870 her last little son, Noel, was born, but lived only a fortnight. Soon after, Maria herself gave up the fight, though tenderly nursed by Louise Desgraz. Maria understood from Hudson's face and words that she was not going to get better on this earth. She left messages for all her dear ones, then she put her thin arms round Hudson's neck, kissed him and fell into her last sleep.

Wrote Hudson, 'her ransomed spirit entered into the joy of the Lord.'

Maria was thirty-three years old, a victim of disease, climate and of twelve years of unremitting labour in giving birth to and caring for her big family, as well as remorselessly undertaking her missionary duties. She had been a true partner for Hudson and now she was gone. Hudson turned to God in his sorrow.

'God comforted my poor heart,' he wrote.

Mercifully the mission station was full of young life and the young couples and lively girls and vigorous men with their enthusiasms and zest for life took Hudson out of himself.

And to keep him company in his inner loneliness was his youngest living boy, little Charlie, two years old. Brief times spent with Charlie brought relief and deep joy to Hudson.

8

New Joys and Renewal

During the following five years, the work of the China Inland Mission was greatly blessed. 'The Lord is prospering us,' wrote Hudson to his mother and father. He went on to point out the importance of the Chinese Christian workers.

'I look on foreign missionaries,' he said 'as the scaffolding round a rising building; the sooner it can be dispensed with the better.' He also thought the Chinese workers should work where they lived, so that the dialect they spoke would be easily understood by those round them.

All this did not stop him asking God to send out more workers from England. The work was expanding. When they had begun the work inland, there had been two mission stations in China and seven church members; now there were thirteen settled stations and thirty workers, on an average, one hundred miles apart.

In England, Mr and Mrs Berger were getting on in years and feeling they must soon retire from managing the Mission's business affairs. Hudson felt he was briefly needed in England to see to things and also of course to renew acquaintance with his growing family, who saw so little of him.

New personal joy came to Hudson. The friendship he and Maria had enjoyed with Jennie Faulding, one of their most lively workers, now blossomed for him into love. Vivacious Jennie, known to the Chinese as 'Miss Happiness', had shown sympathy and support for Hudson in his bereavement and he now felt the time had come when he could ask her to be his wife. She understood the kind of life before her and had no fears.

She loved Hudson, though she was some years younger, and she entered eagerly into married life. In England, Hudson brought her together with his children, his 'darling treasures' and during the next few years, Jennie would have two children of her own.

In place of the Bergers, a Council of Christian Friends was formed, to look after the management of the Mission and recruit new workers. Hudson could leave England with a light heart. The Mission headquarters moved from the Bergers' stately mansion to a modest house in Newington Green, on the outskirts of London and for twenty years this was to be famous as the CIM home base.

*   *   *   *   *   *

Back in China, the mission work was now on a large scale and needed a lot of time spent on administration. Still in charge, Hudson had to face recurring problems; sickness among the staff, shortages of money and equipment, a certain amount of grumbling amongst one or two of the workers and the constant need to encourage people. Hudson and Jennie took everything to God in prayer and answers came; personal difficulties were mostly ironed out.

Hudson and Jennie were now at the zenith of their evangelising life and were constantly travelling. They packed quickly for their simple needs and were off – perhaps to encourage lonely workers, perhaps to open up new districts. They received a warm welcome in their old home at Hangchow, where Pastor Wang was doing marvels.

They set out on a huge task, to visit every one of their stations – places where little churches had been formed. Hudson was never physically robust, yet they walked many miles. They travelled for long journeys by wheelbarrow, pushed by Chinese servants, or swung in sedan mountain chairs, or made trips by the waterways. They were forced to pass through lonely and often dangerous country, but they would not be deterred. They sought out and encouraged all the Chinese workers, the evangelists, the bible carriers called 'colporteurs', the teachers and bible-instructors. Everywhere they went Hudson's medical knowledge and his medicines and instruments were in demand. All these, of course, had to be carried with them, as well as bibles and leaflets. They spent nine months in the valley of the great River Yangtze, then turned their attention to the southern stations in the province of Chekiang.

In 1874, Hudson and Jennie, in their prayers, laid a bold claim before God. They pleaded in prayer for between fifty and one hundred extra Chinese evangelists to take the gospel to the four big towns and forty-eight smaller ones still untouched in Chekiang, and for men to break into the nine unoccupied provinces as yet unvisited. They dared to ask all this in the Name of Jesus.

Funds suddenly got very low. 'All we have,' said Hudson at this point, 'is twenty-five cents . . . and all the promises of God.' Almost immediately, Jennie came into some money and the crisis was over.

*　　*　　*　　*　　*　　*

Another trip to England became necessary. Their dearly-loved friend Emily had died, she who had so lovingly cared for the children. New arrangements now needed to be made. Jennie could not be spared from the work in China that only she could do. So the Taylor children were now added to the brood belonging to Hudson's sister Amelia and her husband. 'If Jennie is called to work for Christ, I am called to look after Jennie's children', said Amelia.

Just before they returned to England, Hudson had had an accident on a small boat, falling and hurting his back. He thought little of it at the time, but as the months went by, and jogging all over England in poorly sprung transport on bad roads, he suffered more and more. Finally he found himself almost completely paralyzed and had to take to his bed at Newington Green. He was furious with himself, but it was no use; to bed he had to go. He pinned up large map of China at the foot of his bed.

Hudson was depressed. How could he conduct the Mission's business from his bed? Well, he just had to. In December 1874 he felt really low – Hudson was always prey to his feelings – and Mission affairs seemed to have reached rock-bottom. Because of the bad publicity issuing from the Yangtze riot affair, and the false accusations about the behaviour of the missionaries, public sympathy for their work diminished for a while and donations merely trickled in instead of coming steadily. Funds for 'forward work' were getting dangerously low.

Bad news also came from China. Grave disturbances had taken place in Huzhou, Suzhou and Ruichang and some American missionaries had been insulted and brutally beaten, while Chinese evangelists had been threatened by the scholar-gentry and chased off. Another wave of anti-foreign feeling!

Hudson began to think it very unlikely that he would ever see China again. It was now almost ten years since the formation of the China Inland Mission. Was its tenth anniversary to be celebrated in despair?

After Christmas, Hudson began to feel better in health and his spirits rose too. He wrote an article which was to have far-reaching effects and which carried in several Christian papers and magazines. This was headed: 'An appeal for prayer on behalf of more than one hundred and fifty millions of Chinese.'

This asked boldly for more workers to go out to China to take the Gospel message to the nine unvisited provinces, each as large as a European kingdom.

The year was not a promising one for such an appeal. A British Consul, Raymond Margary, was killed whilst trying to enter the western provinces of China through Burma. Hudson had also been thinking about this route, believing it to be the most satisfactory way of getting into this area of China, though it would mean traversing high passes and soaring rapids. Even the death of Margary did not daunt him.

He had prayed for eighteen fine strong men to come forward to enter the untapped provinces. Already two such had been accepted, John Stevenson and Henry Soltau. God was heeding the prayers of His people.

Those who called for interview at Newington Green could not fail to notice the utter simplicity of the household; also the childlike nature of the prayers Hudson offered from his sick-bed. Yet they never doubted his authority and power. He always made quite clear what he required from his workers and they knew life would not be a bed of roses. His words rang clearly, 'If you want hard work and little appreciation of it; value God's approbation more than you fear men's disapprobation; are prepared, if need be, to seal your testimony with your blood, and perhaps oftentimes to take joyfully the spoiling of your goods, you may count on a harvest of souls here.'

The China Inland Mission was plainly no place for weaklings or shirkers or anyone who could not go, trusting only in God. Yet young adventurous loving Christian men and women continued to offer themselves.

The money situation eased and some large sums rolled in. One day a Russian nobleman, Count Brobinsky, who bumped into Hudson at a railway station, passed Hudson a bank-note saying, 'Please allow me to give you a trifle towards your work.' Hudson was surprised to see that the note was for £50, a large amount in those days.

'I think this may be a mistake,' he said, showing it to the Count. The Count did look a trifle taken aback. 'Well,' he admitted, 'It's true I meant to give you five pounds, but obviously God meant me to give more. I cannot take it back – please keep it.'

The Mission's work was still supported by donations – gifts – not by subscriptions. There was no begging for funds, only requests for prayers. The Mission, stated Hudson, 'had no paid helpers, only God-led volunteers.' In this, they worked on a different principle from the other missionary societies. Many thought them deranged or stupid, but the necessary monies always came in time.

Hudson got ready to return to China. The situation between England and China was delicate. Families were very worried. But at last the Chinese Foreign Office, the 'Zongli Yamen', realised what a lot of trouble they had caused, and for the time being there was greater calm.

In 1876 the China Inland Mission was ten years old and ready for further growth. Where eighteen workers had been sought, twenty had applied and exciting, daunting tasks were ready for the new team.

9

The Missionary Women

The image of missionary women has often cast them in the mould of Miss Aldersey of Ningbo; getting on in years, stern, somewhat unbending, though faithful, determined and full of good works. Yet Miss Aldersey herself had once been a young worker, who had learned Chinese from the famous missionary translator Robert Morrison.

Enthusiasm for women workers in the field was altogether limited. The Chinese Foreign Office tried to get rid of them. Certainly, when Hudson Taylor took his party out to China on the *Lammermuir* in 1866, there was not one unmarried woman missionary away from the Treaty Ports in the whole of China.

It was unusual for unmarried ladies to be accepted by the missionary societies. The Church Missionary Society was quite coy on the subject. Nor would this have been though well of in general society. To send single girls to work with a lot of young men! To send single girls to work on their own and in tense areas! Mad, bad, and dangerous; this was the common view.

Yet Hudson followed the principles of the Dutch missionary Charles Gutzlaff, who had always believed in the 'value of pious females' and had himself married the first single Protestant woman missionary to East Asia. Hudson believed that women could serve usefully in China, particularly in getting close to Chinese women, for whom on the whole he felt very sorry. 'Do love the Chinese women', he always urged.

He adhered to his own view and ignored criticism. So also must the young ladies whom he accepted; they had to know what the reaction would be to them, and be prepared for it.

Only time and experience showed how valuable these young women proved to be and how much of the successful work of the Mission could never have taken place without them.

Most acceptable were the missionary wives. The young men, if not already married when they sailed, did their utmost to find a wife quickly. In what seems a rather cold-blooded manner, they wrote home to girls they had perhaps met only a few times, asking for their hand. For many reasons, a suitable wife was important for the missionary men. And if, as too often happened, the wife died within a few years, they rapidly sought another.

Not all could measure up to the standard of Maria and Jennie Taylor. Hudson wrote quite severely of the requirements of missionary wives:

'They might be expected to make some little progress in the language before marrying and thus could have a fair chance of future usefulness . . .

if these conditions seem too hard . . . do not join our mission . . .'

This blunt comment was probably for the good of the wives. If they married and went to China expecting a cossetted life, they were in for a big disappointment. They must be hardy and inwardly strong, confident in their Christian faith and in themselves, relying upon God but capable of taking their share in the missionary work, perhaps teaching or visiting. Maria was well-known for discouraging any fastidious attitudes towards food or fashion!

All this must be as well as running the home, overseeing the Chinese servants, and, never to be forgotten, bearing the large families of Victorian times, sometimes as many as ten children.

Much of Hudson Taylor's programme of travels was determined by the confinements of the ladies of the mission staff. Since they could not afford the services of the Foreign Settlement doctor, and were often too far away in any case, Hudson must attend them all and spent a good deal of time delivering babies, which activity had to be fitted into his itinerary.

With medicine and antenatal care still primitive and with problems of climate, many of the babies, children and mothers did not live long. Hudson's friend Edward Lord lost two wives in China, as did Jim Meadows.

All this the mettlesome girls thought worthwhile. But it was no joke to go out to China to be a missionary wife, though one might gain respect and affection. It could be downright dangerous, when waves of anti-foreign feeling swept the land. When the wives wore Chinese clothing, as they had agreed to do, their movements were even more limited, as they had also to conform to Chinese etiquette, which for some was very irksome indeed. No more jumping about or running in public!

As well as Hudson's two wives, many married women played a considerable part in the progress of the CIM, Mrs Lord, Mrs Bausum, from missionary families, were strong and useful. Grace Ciggie was a young Scotswoman who worked in the 'red light' district of the Glasgow Salt Market, where she was much loved. She had little education but much zeal. George Stott, whom she knew only very slightly, wrote from China asking her to marry him. She accepted and was the last of the CIM workers to travel to China by sailing ship. Usually these girls were sent with an escort to chaperone them but none could be found for Grace. She therefore travelled alone and was unperturbed. On arrival in China, she was soon married to George and whisked off to a rough and ready home in Wenzhou, the first foreign woman ever to be seen there. It was a tough, lonely assignment.

A thousand miles up the River Yangtze George Nicoll and his wife reached Chunking, in the enormous province of Szechwan, where Mrs Nicoll was the only foreign woman. She found herself mobbed, in a friendly way, by Chinese women. 'For nearly two months past, she wrote, 'I have daily seen hundreds of women. Our house has been like a fair . . .'

George and Mrs Clarke travelled even further,

another seventeen days of tiring journey, to the capital of Kweichow, a distant point. Mrs Clarke then went on to a still more remote and difficult province in Yunnan. Her work here bore much fruit. In the two churches where she was a pioneer, a church numbering more than eight thousand people spread across to Burma in time to come.

A younger missionary and his very young wife, Mr and Mrs Botham, set of as a kind of 'caravan' mission, intending not to stop in one place but to visit a parish of twenty-two governing cities, sixty market towns and numerous villages. They went by themselves and set off simply on donkey back.

One or two women found they just could not stand the life and wisely returned home. Mrs Cardwell was one such; she could not get on with the Chinese clothing and disliked the Chinese people.

When Hudson took out the *Lammermuir* party, this included seven young unmarried women, all in their twenties. No wonder there was much tutt-tutting and a certain amount of scandalous talk in the first stages of their ministry. These girls had all been carefully selected from those who applied and there was hardly a failure. They were very different from one another, some had been teachers and governesses and were comparatively well-educated, some were of lesser education but practical, sincere Christians with differing skills. Secretarial training was very useful as Hudson was a business-like person and wanted careful accounts kept and correspondence filed.

The girls had differing temperaments too. Maira was strong, quiet and calm. She had been born and grew up in the Far East and spoke perfect Mandarin. Jennie was vivacious and bustling. Emily Blatchley was domesticated and affectionate, known to Hudson as 'Aim-mee', dearest sister. Louise Desgraz, a Swiss, formerly a governess was a tender nurse. She was sensitive and was deeply disturbed by the sight of Chinese worshipping idols and many other things that offended her. But she was a great encourager.

'But for her,' wrote Hudson, 'the Chinese Christians of Zhenjang would have given up.'

Henrietta Soltau longed to go out to China, but Hudson, from his experience, thought she was not physically strong enough. So she worked busily at the home-base in England and later became recognised as the training person for young ladies going out East.

Many of these young women eventually found themselves alone in isolated outposts and bore themselves with bravery and authority. In a complete chain of ten central missions and sixty outposts, women were the only foreign missionaries. They were usually greatly respected. In the time of a fierce riot in Szechwan, some women missionaries shared a house in a lonely hill station. Unknown to them, a rota of Christian Chinese men stayed outside their house each night to guard them, untill the danger had passed.

Mrs McCarthy, working in Kweiyang, wrote home: 'We find people most friendly – we go in and out without the least inconvenience. As we walk about, we get many invitations to sit down and drink tea.' Even crossing the desperately anti-foreign province of Hunan, Miss Kidd could write of 'friendly women wanting to detain them.'

Chinese people were puzzled by the presence in public of unmarried lady workers, but felt on easy terms with Miss Elizabeth Wilson in Hangchung-Fu. Miss Wilson was a lady in her fifties with pretty silvery hair. Since they honour older people, the Chinese respected Elizabeth and grew to love her, the women tottering along on their tiny bound feet to call on 'Elder sister'.

It was dramatic when Jennie Taylor, the only possible person of sufficient experience, dashed in 1877 to North China where a terrible famine was causing sorrow and loss of life. She hurried to Shansi – no foreign woman had ever before tried to go so far into the interior. She was able to organise practical relief work and found an orphanage, as well as giving spiritual instruction and comfort.

And Miss Jacobsen agreed to try and settle in Hunan, the 'Iron Gate, for long the most anti-foreign and dangerous province in the whole of China. In her Chinese clothes, she walked demurely over the border under the eyes of the guard, who did not recognise a dreaded 'foreigner' in this quietly-moving dusty traveller.

Hudson accepted that he was unconventional in commissioning young ladies and he did his best to look after them. Where should they live? He often put them together to share a house, so as to offend neither the Chinese nor the Settlement community, nor indeed the girls' families.

There is no evidence that the girls regretted offering, though many suffered and some died. Emily King, the first woman to enter Western China, died of of typhus in 1881, far from family and friends. Yet she had seen eighteen Chinese women baptized in her brief ministry.

A special prayer-union was formed in England to seek God's blessing on the one hundred and twenty-five million women in China who had not heard of Jesus Christ. Those who responded may have known hard, sometimes brief lives, but they could never complain of lack of excitement, interest and results.

10

Go, Go, Go!

When Hudson Taylor returned to China in 1876, he was very much aware of the simmering aftermath of the troubles over the murder of Consul Margary. However, an important gathering at Chefoo had altered much. The doors had now been thrown open of access for foreigners to the remotest parts of China. According to the Imperial edict, foreigners could now travel freely and safely in any part of the Emperor's domain. Notices to this effect were being posted in every town and city. It was 'friendly to foreigners' time!

Hudson was overjoyed. God be praised! Here was the opportunity he had always sought; the right to go anywhere in China to speak for Christ. He was now experienced in understanding the Chinese way of thinking and he believed the new proclamation might not last. But for now, here was the golden chance. It should, for the Mission, be immediately – go, go, go!

Like greyhounds released, the workers went. Backwards and forwards across China they travelled, in conditions of hardship and health hazard and occasional danger. They were young and keen, their hearts were light. For the most part, the selectors at home and Hudson himself, had chosen well. All he had asked was that they be dedicated followers of Christ; he did not care to what denomination they belonged.

What did the volunteers, on their side, see when they first met Hudson? One wrote that they saw 'what looked like a Chinaman on a barrow, almost as broad as long, in padded gown and jacket and face covered over with a wind hood, only nose and eyes showing.' The writer added, 'and grasping a large Chinese umbrella in true native style, with the handle pointing foremost!'

Hudson often played a little trick on male newcomers, but for a purpose. He wanted to see what they were made of, so he first of all put them up in a typical earth-floored Chinese inn. Here they faced simplicity to the point of roughness, in sleeping, living and eating. And of course the stare of every Chinese eye.

Mostly, the excited youngsters did not care at all. They wrote home, 'we took to Chinese dress, food, ways, like a duck to water.'

Hudson was blessed with strong, keen workers and he set them some daunting tasks. Yet they were always volunteering to go further and deeper into the interior of China.

He wrote to England, 'I trust there be no county left in this province in which we have not preached Christ. There are fifty cities still to be possessed for Christ.'

The great map of China which he was constantly

studying was now criss-crossed with pencil marks as one after another new provinces were entered. James Cameron traversed every province in China except Hunan, even reaching Mongolia and Tibet. George Clarke and Edward Fisher went still further south in untouched country to Kwangsi. Broumton visited every city in Eastern Yunnan. And Stevenson and Soltau were the first Europeans to travel from the Burma frontier right through China to Shanghai on the coast.

There were still difficulties; places so remote that the Imperial edict had not reached them. Places where the Mandarins were unfriendly and the people hostile. But for the most part, there was a rising tide of spiritual blessing and the young missionaries were heard with respect and their Christian Chinese scriptures accepted.

A vast organization now existed which needed funds. Hudson still did not ask the home society to beg for funds, but to pray for necessary monies, and to tell of their doings in print. Soon, prayer groups were boldly asking God for a few large gifts, rather than a lot of little ones, to keep down the secretarial book-keeping work! To Hudson's unashamed delight, eleven thousand pounds was donated – in just eleven payments.

Hudson was overjoyed at the opportunities presented and taken. The next pressing problem was how to raise and maintain settled churches in the places now being opened up by the evangelists.

He still worked relentlessly and brooded over problems, though often now he could be heard to say that he 'whistled and rolled his burden on to the Lord'. But his strength was taxed, he was not getting any younger, and he was forced to take several short breaks. After a nasty attack of dysentery, he went to spend a short holiday in the bracing northern sea port of Chefoo, on a peninsula sticking out into the Yellow Sea. This was a quiet place, with yellow sands and freshwater streams inland.

As Hudson felt better, he began to think of what a wonderful place Chefoo would be for a holiday home for weary workers and their children, or even a hospital and sanatorium for sick missionaries – and perhaps an orphanage. To his surprise, a farmer came up and asked 'Do you want to buy a bean-field?' There and then the matter was settled. Hudson and his colleague Charlie Judd found workmen to quarry stone, make bricks and use ships' beams for doors, floors and furniture. Thus arose a simple building which became the first school for CIM children.

Hudson wrote to his mother, 'the work is extending and consolidating . . . it is worth living and dying for . . .'

The CIM was now twenty years old and had seen some tremendous successes and awakenings. Hudson began to feel there must be a price to pay and in his bones began to expect trouble. So many new ideas were now abroad in China, so many old habits turned round, there must surely be a reaction, even if God had been involved all along. He hoped and prayed that when the time came, they would all stand firm.

11

The Progress and The Price

A burst of anti-foreign feeling resulted in riots in the Yangzte Valley. This made Hudson uneasy. Troubles beset the Mission. Workers became ill and some died. One became mentally ill and had to be constantly watched and cared for. One or two of the younger workers made mistakes and upset people.

Yet new mission centres were being opened. Hudson now placed the day to day work in the hands of a younger man and introduced John Stevenson as his deputy.

John had been thinking of the scripture passage: 'The Lord appointed another seventy'. John encouraged friends to pray for one hundred new workers. Then, in their moment of widest outlook, Hudson and John thought – if a hundred, why not a thousand? They visualised the enormous population of China and saw a simple solution:

'A million is a thousand thousand. Given a thousand evangelists each teaching two hundred and fifty people daily, in one thousand days two hundred and fifty millions would have the offer of Divine mercy!'

This task could be carried out in just a little over three years and should not be beyond the resources of the Christian Church.

Even Hudson was staggered at this idea, yet it seemed to him perfectly reasonable, and with God's help, possible. This noble ideal was set out in a book called *China's Millions* and this bore results. Hudson always stressed, though, that they wanted 'no loiterers' – only hard workers should apply.

The next step was for Hudson to take this appeal to a wider audience. He was persuaded to travel abroad to share with other Christian nations his concern for China. It was again remarked that he was not of imposing appearance, but his speeches, though quiet and simple, really hit home.

So convinced were Hudson and John that God would heed their plea for more workers, that they held a special thanksgiving service even before the workers started to apply.

A distinguished missionary, Dr Harold Schofield, died of fever. Beforehand he had prayed to God to raise up a group of men and women of high education and natural talents; he believed that these were now specifically needed by the Mission. Almost immediately after his death a group of seven men offered themselves for missionary work. They were graduates from Cambridge University and were known as 'the Cambridge Seven'. They included a young Royal Artillery Officer called DE Hoste, and CT Studd, a well-known gentleman cricketer. These young men were handsome, healthy and bright, and were known as the 'athletic missionaries'. They quickly inspired other university types to offer for the CIM and brought a valuable element into the band of workers.

Hudson's overseas visits also bore fruit. An American called Henry Frost and his family sold their home and took up a post in Canada to work for the CIM making a decision to live by faith, as the CIM did. Since they had lived in rather princely style, this was a hard decision to make. Young Americans in numbers applied to go to China and sixty from Australia and fifty from Sweden. All quarters of the world were now ringing with tales of the CIM and responding to the call.

At times, money shortages arose but were short-lived. Hudson would say, with a smile, 'Now you will see what God will do.'

China now began to enter on a troubled period. She was moving from centuries of isolation to having to accept a place in the great family of nations. She did not find this easy, having thought of herself for so long as the centre of the earth.

The Manchu dynasty in Peking grew weak and forces of disorder broke loose. Secret societies arose and there were angry meetings. In an upsurge of the religion of Islam, which some Chinese followed, Muslims swept down on the city of Sining, on the border of Tibet, and fought their own compatriots.

This was unnerving to the missionaries there, Mr and Mrs Ridley, and their child, the only foreigners. Terrible bloodshed occurred. Led by an informant, the missionaries made their way to a temple where they found hundreds of wounded women and children.

The Ridleys realised that they were needed and must not try to escape. With only penknives and a razor, they performed operations and bound up wounds.

Relief troops were slow to come. Smallpox was rampant in the city and food was scarce. In the winter that lasted seven months, the temperature was often below zero. It was a time of challenge. The Ridleys found they had been spared; a friendly Mandarin smuggled grain to them. It was two years before the city was relieved and eighty thousand people were killed in the fighting or died of cold.

Hudson, far away in Shanghai, was very worried when he heard of all this. News came of riots, persecution and rebellion, from the coast right across China to the borders of Tibet. A few sparks had set the country alight. In Chengtu, capital of Szechwan, mission property was burned down. In Wenchow, one of the longest-founded Christian places, homes were attacked and looted and long years of work undone. The Rev Robert Steward, his wife and child and eight workers of the Church Missionary Society were murdered.

Hudson knew personal sorrow. Some of his best friends had died of cholera, the dreaded disease that stalked these days. One thing cheered him greatly. No lives had been lost in Szechwan and when order was restored, it was found that most of the Chinese Christians had faithfully stood their ground.

These were indeed the fearful days that Hudson had foreseen. Not only was the Christian faith being tested by its life-changing character, but the unstable nature of Chinese political life now was bound to bring problems. No one seemed to be in charge.

Yet Hudson noted that, in the year 1895, with all its sorrows and terrors, marvellous signs and wonders had occurred. The prayer of Hudson and John Stevenson for a thousand workers had been answered.

In fact, over eleven hundred people had volunteered and were accepted for further missionary work, despite the tales that must have filtered back to England of affairs in China.

The young workers had evolved a useful pattern of activity for times of hostility. They left the area quietly, worked their way round the country in a circle, and then came back to try again.

Also, pointed out Hudson proudly, despite everything, a larger number of converts had been baptised that year than in any previous year in the history of the Mission.

God's will could not be overruled by evil events.

12

Handing On

Foreign pressure continued upon China. In a war with Japan, from 1894-1951, she was defeated. She realised how the adoption of western ways could increase the fighting power of an oriental nation. Intelligent Chinese people began to realise the need for change, for reform inside China. They saw their country lose Korea to Japan, Port Arthur to Russia. Reforms must begin.

But these big changes, begun by advisers to the young Emperor, galvanised to fury the ambitious Dowager Empress, Ci Xi. She seized the reins of government, imprisoned the Emperor, executed many of the Court and officials, and said no to all reforms. Those that had already taken place, she abolished.

There were now plans to reverse the policies of more recent years. Once again, foreigners were the enemies and their pretensions should be discouraged.

In the midst of all this turbulence, Hudson and Jennie undertook their last period of active service in China. They were calm but anxious. God had protected the mission and its servants for over thirty years. Even now, despite all the dangers, two hundred and fifty people had been received as Christians on the Kwangsin River.

Hudson and Jennie were not bothered about themselves. Their children were grown up and much involved in CIM work. They did fear for the safety of the workers and their flocks. There were signs of new persecution of Christians. Now took place the first martyrdom in the CIM. Australian worker William Fleming was murdered, with his friend and Chinese helper, P'An.

Though not well, Hudson was still travelling round the world speaking on behalf of the Mission. While in Australia, he heard the most dread news of all, coming from China. The Empress Ci Xi had issued a proclamation which was brutal in its bareness, 'All foreigners should be killed.' As most foreigners were missionaries, they were to bear the brunt.

Hudson was terribly upset. His health suffered and for several weeks he could not work. That it should come to this! Gangs of Chinese, members of secret societies called 'Boxers', were rampaging round the country, murdering anyone not a Chinese. They showed no mercy. Hundreds of Christians were massacred and refugees from other countries hunted down. There were riots and fighting and the Foreign Legations – buildings representing foreign countries – were in a state of siege; their staffs were unable to go in or out and food became scarce. It was a time of terror.

Poor Hudson, in his low state, said, 'I cannot read, I cannot think, I cannot even pray – but I can trust.' He felt there just had soon to be an end to this madness.

Finally, united foreign troops marched into China and entered Peking and the court fled. The European powers dicated severe terms. Fortifications were destroyed, apologies demanded, and large sums of money sought as reparation. Again China felt humiliated. But at last the Boxer menace subsided and a kind of normality began to creep back.

Many had suffered during these years and the China Inland Mission had a martyr roll of fifty members killed, including twenty-one children, victims of Ci Xi.

Yet, despite all this, the letters that went backwards and forwards from China to England showed that the members of the mission were amazingly free of bitterness. They talked little of their own fears and sufferings. When the European nations demanded an awful vengeance from China, Hudson Taylor advised the British Foreign Office that he and his workers would not be seeking money by way of compensation. He seemed to be saying 'It was all a time of passing madness.'

The British Foreign Office was amazed at this attitude. Our Minister in Peking, a high British official, sent a private donation to Hudson in 'admiration and sympathy'. The Christian stand adopted by Hudson and the Mission members had really been noticed. There were to be no demands for revenge from the CIM.

* * * * * *

All this took a toll of Hudson, even though he was not actually in China at the height of the troubles. He had worried so much that he had made himself ill. He was now nearly seventy and feeling weary. Plans were made for Hudson and Jennie to go to Switzerland, where they always felt better and they went to live in a quiet hamlet by the Lake of Geneva, near their friends the Bergers. Hudson had to come to terms with the knowledge that his hectic days might be over. He and Jennie knew a quiet happiness together; they walked arm in arm in the flower-scented fields by day and studied the stars at night.

Hudson had officially appointed as Director to follow him, D E Hoste, one of the 'Cambridge Seven.' It was left to Hudson to exercise a ministry of prayer and letter-writing. He felt bad at not being in the thick of things. 'It's hardest of all to do nothing for His sake', he muttered. This made Jennie smile. She was very glad to have him to herself. It was not to be for long.

A year or so later, came the end of Jennie's earthly life. She died very peacefully, her last words being, 'My grace is sufficient.' She had been a true and active helpmeet for Hudson for thirty-three years, and in spite of their many separations, he felt a great emptiness without her. 'Miss Happiness' had gone.

Hudson grew stronger in the Swiss air and enjoyed the company of his neice, Mary Broomhall. He was so much better that he decided to return to his beloved China, instead of just sitting there in Switzerland. He travelled by way of America, with his son and daughter-in-law. They landed in Shanghai in April 1905.

It was fifty-three years since he had first set foot on Chinese soil here. They began a nostalgic tour, meeting the new Director, and as many as could be fitted in of the friends of time past. Everywhere Hudson went there were flowers in his room and beautiful scarlet satin banners with the words 'Welcome, O man beloved'.

They spent Easter at Yangchow, where the riot had occured. Then on to the new Mission house at Chinkiang. From here Hudson walked privately to the little cemetery overlooking the river where lay his first wife, Maria, and four of their children. Only he knew what thoughts then passed through his mind.

He longed to go again into the interior and they made use of the new railway which ran all the way to Peking. Hudson remembered with a smile the long journey this way he once undertaken by wheelbarrow. That had not been at all comfortable.

They spent a night at a village inn and now it seemed quite a strange experience. They visited five centres in Hona and everywhere Hudson had a right royal welcome.

Their last journey was to the city of Changsa, by steamer. This was the capital of Hunan which for so many years had resisted the Christian presence. As they went up the river and passed cities and plains, the ripening crops and the noble mountains, Hudson's heart was full.

His thoughts turned to the Chinese converts who had made the 'Forward movement' possible. They had all followed in the steps of Liang-A-Fa, the engraver of Canton, the first Chinese Protestant Pastor, before Hudson's day, who for his newfound faith had endured flogging, mobbing and betrayal.

There were the Pastors whom Hudson had brought into service, above all dear Wang Le-Djun, pastor and friend, and the hymnwriter, Pastor Hsi, a graduate of Shansi, and the husband of a very special wife.

Hsi and his wife longed to take the Gospel to the city of Hwochow, but lacked the money. Mrs Hsi gave up her personal jewellery to raise cash – the important items of her marriage dowry. 'I can do without these,' she said, 'let Hwochow have the Gospel.' There was also Pastor Wang Guoya, an ebullient evangelist, never down for long. He had cared for years for the Fenghua outstations.

Hudson thought of outstanding Chinese Christians from ordinary backgrounds, whose lives had been altered by their acceptance of Jesus Christ: Feng Nenggui, the basket maker; Ling Zhumou the cook. Captain Yu of the Imperial Army. The Captain was so impressed by the Gospel story that he had offered to preach for nothing. And he in his turn had influenced Farmer Tung, later to be a most successful evangelist.

Then there were the young victims of outrage, adopted as family by Hudson and Maria, Tong Tianxi, a destitute Shanghai boy, and Tsiu Kyou-Kwe, an orphan girl.

A whole roll-call of names flashed through Hudson's mind as he steamed up the river; Chinese Christians of enduring faith and courage.

They reached Changsa in June and Hudson was taken by sedan chair to a lofty building on the highest point of the city wall; he had always loved looking out over great China.

A reception was held for him in a cool and pleasant garden and friends old and new crowded round. They were all excited to see him. Hudson gave a blessing to the workers and a special message for young missionaries.

'The Lord Jesus will never leave us nor forsake us. Count on Him . . . enjoy Him . . . be true to Him . . . He will never disappoint you . . .' It was obvious to all that he spoke from the heart and from all his years of experience in this beloved land. It was hard for Hudson to tear himself away. And hard for the people to let him go. To some who had never met him before, he was the legendary leader.

At last his daughter-in-law hurried him off. He was looking tired and she was a little worried. He went to bed early, happy and content. He had some letters from England to read.

Shortly afterwards, his daughter-in-law looked into his room with some supper. There was stillness. As she bent over him, she realised he was no longer breathing. Hudson had passed peacefully into the nearer presence of the God he loved. The long years of service, in this world, had ended.

'The weight of years seemed to pass away; he looked like a child quietly sleeping', said those who saw him.

There was great sorrow when everyone heard of Hudson's passing but also great rejoicing for such a life. Hudson was buried alongside his Maria and four of their family, near the river, in the China that he loved. At his funeral, little round-faced Chinese children sang in their high sweet voices and brought flowers to honour him.

People from all over the world sent messages of condolence and appreciation. Said one, 'His was the heart-beat felt throughout the Mission.'

They all remembered the few words that summed up the life of this Yorkshire boy:

'If I had a thousand pounds China should have it; if I had a thousand lives, China should have them. No! Not China, but Christ – can we do too much for him?'